ICONS

SYDNEY STYLE

SYDNEY

Exteriors   Interiors

STYLE

Details

PHOTOS **Giorgio Possenti/Vega MG**

EDITOR **Angelika Taschen**

TASCHEN

KÖLN LONDON LOS ANGELES MADRID PARIS TOKYO

PHOTOGRAPHIC CREDITS   CRÉDITS PHOTOGRAPHIQUES   BILDNACHWEIS

© 2003 for the works by Roy Lichtenstein, Ludwig Mies van der Rohe, Jean Nouvel, Frank Stella:
VG Bild-Kunst, Bonn

© 2003 for the works by Le Corbusier: FLC/VG Bild-Kunst, Bonn

© 2003 for the works by Charles and Ray Eames: Lucia Eames dba Eames Office, P.O. Box 268,
USA Venice, CA 90294, www.eamesoffice.com

Also available from TASCHEN:

Living in Sydney
200 pages
3–8228–1384-2

© 2004 TASCHEN GmbH
Hohenzollernring 53, D–50672 Köln
www.taschen.com

Concept and layout by Angelika Taschen, Cologne
Cover design by Angelika Taschen, Claudia Frey, Cologne
General project management by Stephanie Bischoff, Cologne
Texts by Christiane Reiter, Berlin
Lithography by Tina Ciborowius, Cologne
English translation by Catherine Lara, Berlin
French translation by Anne Charrière, Croissy/Seine

Printed in Spain
ISBN 3–8228–3229–4

CONTENTS SOMMAIRE INHALT

It's one of those days in Sydney when you know, from the very moment you wake up, that it's going to be perfect. The sun casts a velvety soft glow in the room; between the slats of the wooden Venetian blinds, sky blue and jungle green sparkle with an intensity that is normally common only to tropical islands, and inside one can even sense the light fragrance of sand and salt that fills the air outside. A day like this simply has to be spent by the sea, for it's to the Pacific that Sydney owes its airiness and its unique light – even the wind is said to have its own colour here. The Pacific makes Sydney a city of the senses – though not one for dreamy romantics: here, on the east coast of Australia, no one is content to cast longing glances at the CinemaScopic coastline and the glittering

CITY OF THE SENSES
Christiane Reiter

Le jour se lève sur Sydney, une journée dont on sait dès le réveil qu'elle sera parfaite. Magique, un reflet de soleil satiné colore la pièce. Entre les lamelles des jalousies en bois, un bleu de ciel et un vert de forêt vierge étincellent avec une intensité tropicale, et le léger parfum de sable et de sel qui flotte dans l'air extérieur se pressent aussi au dedans. Une telle journée est faite pour aller à la mer ; car c'est au Pacifique que Sydney doit sa légèreté et sa lumière exceptionnelle – même le vent aurait ici des couleurs particulières... Le Pacifique fait de Sydney une ville sensuelle – mais pas pour de romantiques rêveurs : ici, sur la côte est de l'Australie, personne ne se contente de jeter des regards langoureux sur une plage hollywoodienne et une mer étincelante – les habitants ne vivent pas seulement au bord de l'eau mais aussi avec elle. Quelle cave, quel placard à vêtement

Es ist einer jener Tage in Sydney, an dem man schon beim Aufwachen weiß, dass er perfekt werden wird. Die Sonne zaubert einen samtweichen Schimmer in den Raum, zwischen den Lamellen der Holzjalousien blitzen Himmelblau und Urwaldgrün in einer Intensität, wie sie sonst nur tropische Inseln bieten, und der leichte Duft nach Sand und Salz, der draußen in der Luft liegt, lässt sich sogar im Haus erahnen. Einen solchen Tag muss man am Meer verbringen; denn es ist der Pazifik, dem Sydney seine Leichtigkeit und sein einzigartiges Licht verdankt – sogar der Wind soll hier seine eigenen Farben besitzen. Der Pazifik macht Sydney zu einer Stadt der Sinne – allerdings zu keiner für verträumte Romantiker: Hier, an der Ostküste Australiens, begnügt sich niemand mit sehnsüchtigen Blicken auf die kinotaugliche Küste und das glitzernde Meer – die Menschen

sea – the people don't just live by the sea, but with the sea, too. Surfboards and beachwear made in Australia can be found in almost every cellar or wardrobe; an afternoon at the seaside resort of Manly, a boat trip across the bays of Jackson Port, or surfing on the waves as they break on the beach are part and parcel of everyday life. Perhaps it's because of these multi-coloured leisure pastimes that many houses and apartments are comparatively plain design and construction. They make effective counterpoints: spacious rooms and exquisite furniture, clear forms and few colours, fine materials and amusing or charming details. Sydney offers a perfect merging of inner and outer worlds – and that's something you can enjoy almost every morning anew, at the beginning of a perfect day.

n'héberge pas sa planche de surf, et sa tenue de plage made in Australia ; une après-midi à la station balnéaire de Manly, une excursion en barque dans les baies de Jackson Port ou une séance de surf face à la plage font naturellement partie du quotidien. Peut-être ces activités de loisirs chatoyantes expliquent-elles pourquoi beaucoup de maisons et d'appartements à Sydney sont conçus et dessinés avec une telle sobriété. Ces édifices s'érigent en contrepoints éloquents : grandes surfaces, mobilier choisi, formes claires, économie de couleur, matériaux nobles et détails amusants ou charmants. A Sydney, un lien parfait a été tissé entre le monde intérieur et extérieur – jouissance qui se renouvelle presque chaque matin – au commencement d'une journée parfaite.

leben nicht nur am Wasser, sondern mit dem Wasser. Surfbretter und Beachwear made in Australia sind in fast jedem Keller beziehungsweise Kleiderschrank zu finden; ein Nachmittag im Seebad Manly, ein Bootsausflug durch die Buchten von Jackson Port oder Wellenreiten vor den Stränden sind selbstverständliche Bestandteile des Alltags. Vielleicht liegt es an diesem Freizeitprogramm in allen Nuancen des Regenbogens, dass viele Häuser und Wohnungen in Sydney vergleichsweise schlicht entworfen und designt sind. Sie setzen wirkungsvolle Kontrapunkte: weitläufige Grundrisse und ausgesuchte Möbel, klare Formen und wenige Farben, edle Materialien und amüsant-charmante Details. In Sydney gibt es die vollkommene Verbindung von Innen- und Außenwelt – und das genießt man an fast jedem Morgen aufs Neue; am Beginn eines perfekten Tages.

"It was a clear, sunny day with high, white clouds and a breeze blowing off the sea in the direction of the coast. A couple of yachts were sailing out, bound for The Heads."

Bruce Chatwin in *The Songlines*

« La journée était claire, ensoleillée, avec de hauts nuages blancs et une brise qui soufflait de la mer vers la côte. Quelques yachts en partance faisaient voile vers The Heads. »

Bruce Chatwin dans *Le Chant des pistes*

„Es war ein klarer, sonniger Tag mit hohen weißen Wolken und einer Brise, die vom Meer in Richtung der Küste wehte. Ein paar Yachten, die nach draußen segelten, hielten auf The Heads zu."

Bruce Chatwin in *Traumpfade*

EXTERIORS

Regards au dehors Aussichten

10/11 View of the skyline: in the living room of Bay Watch House in Rose Bay. *Vue sur l'horizon : depuis le salon de la maison Bay Watch dans la baie Rose.* Sicht auf die Skyline: Im Wohnzimmer des Bay Watch House an der Rose Bay.

12/13 Next to Harbour Bridge: the penthouse terrace of architect Harry Seidler. *Tout près de Harbour Bridge : la terrasse-penthouse de l'architecte Harry Seidler.* Direkt an der Harbour Bridge: Die Penthouse-Terrasse des Architekten Harry Seidler.

14/15 Holiday atmosphere: pool and palms give a tropical flair. *Atmosphère de vacances : piscine et palmiers créent une impression tropicale.* Urlaubsstimmung: Pool und Palmen sorgen für tropisches Flair.

16/17 The name is binding: Burley Katon Halliday's "waterfront homes" in Elizabeth Bay. *Nom obligé : les « maisons du front de l'eau » de Burley Katon Halliday dans la baie Elizabeth.* Der Name verpflichtet: Burley Katon Hallidays „waterfront homes" an der Elizabeth Bay.

18/19 The beach outside the door: from English House there's a view of Coogee Beach. *La plage devant la porte : depuis la maison English le regard tombe sur la baie Coogee.* Den Strand vor der Tür: Vom English House blickt man auf den Coogee Beach.

20/21 A gate of stone: Two reefs protect Sydney from the high surf of the Pacific. *Une porte dans la roche : deux récifs protègent Sydney des vagues du Pacifique.* Ein Tor aus Fels: Zwei Riffe schützen Sydney vor der Brandung des Pazifiks.

22/23 Fluid transition: Craig Rosevear's Archer House is directly by the sea. *Transition fluide : la maison Archer de Craig Rosevear se dresse face à la mer.* Fließender Übergang: Das Archer House von Craig Rosevear steht direkt am Meer.

24/25 A place in the sun: on the veranda of the Archer House. *Une place au soleil : sur la terrasse de la maison Archer.* Ein Platz an der Sonne: Auf der Veranda des Archer House.

26/27 Perfect panorama: in the Bingley/Pullin House above Chinaman's Beach. *Panorama parfait : dans la maison Bingley/Pullin au-dessus de la baie Chinaman.* Perfektes Panorama: Im Bingley/Pullin House über dem Chinamans Beach.

28/29 Living room in white: "La chaise" and a bird chair in Reynolds House. *Salon en blanc : « La Chaise » et un fauteuil Oiseau dans la maison Reynolds.* Wohnzimmer in Weiß: „La Chaise" und ein Bird-Sessel im Reynolds House.

30/31 Mirror images: in front of Harry Seidler's plainly designed penthouse on Milson's Point. *Images reflets : devant le penthouse aux lignes claires, dessiné par Harry Seidler à Milsons Point.* Spiegelbilder: Vor Harry Seidlers klar designtem Penthouse am Milsons Point.

"Again and again you caught a glimpse of the port – over a garden wall, at the foot of a sloping street, between two close-set houses – like on a handkerchief that's been put out to dry."

Bill Bryson in *Down Under. In a Sunburned Country*

« De temps en temps apparaissait un coin de port – par-dessus un mur de jardin, au bas d'une rue en pente, entre deux maisons rapprochées – comme sur un linge mis à sécher. »

Bill Bryson dans *Down Under. In a Sunburned Country*

„Immer wieder erwischte man einen Blick auf den Hafen – über eine Gartenmauer, am Fuß einer abfallenden Straße, zwischen zwei nah beieinander stehenden Häusern – wie auf ein Tuch, das zum Trocknen aufgehängt ist."

Bill Bryson in *Frühstück mit Kängurus. Australische Abenteuer*

INTERIORS

Regards au dedans Einsichten

36/37 Weight seems weightless: steel and cement on the first floor of Archer House. *Le lourd paraît léger: fer et ciment au premier étage de la maison Archer.* Schweres wirkt leicht: Eisen und Zement in der ersten Etage des Archer House.

38/39 Contrasts: Black sofas and light-coloured terrace chairs at Archer House. *Contrastes : sofas noirs et chaises claires de terrasse dans la maison Archer.* Kontraste: Schwarze Sofas und helle Terrassenstühle im Archer House.

40/41 Tied up: The "MR" chairs at the Archer House were designed by Ludwig Mies van der Rohe. *Ficelé : les chaises « MR » de la maison Archer House sont signées Ludwig Mies van der Rohe.* Geschnürt: Die Stühle „MR" im Archer House entwarf Ludwig Mies van der Rohe.

42/43 Eye-catcher: the painting "Tree" by John Coburn in the Archer House. *Bien en vue : le tableau « Arbre » de John Coburn dans la maison Archer.* Blickfang: Das Gemälde „Tree" von John Coburn im Archer House.

44/45 Elegant curves: The spiral staircase at Harry Seidler's seems to float. *Elan élégant : l'escalier en colimaçon chez Harry Seidler semble flotter.* Eleganter Schwung: Die Wendeltreppe bei Harry Seidler scheint zu schweben.

46/47 Colour and fur: In the bedroom Harry Seidler gazes at a Lichtenstein painting. *Couleur et peau de fauve : dans la chambre à coucher, Harry Seidler contemple un tableau de Lichtenstein.* Farbe und Fell: Im Schlafzimmer blickt Harry Seidler auf ein Lichtenstein-Gemälde.

48/49 Behind glass: This is how Harry Seidler shows the reclining chair by Le Corbusier to its best advantage. *Derrière la vitre : comment Harry Seidler met en valeur une chaise longue Le Corbusier.* Hinter Glas: So bringt Harry Seidler die Chaiselongue von Le Corbusier zur Geltung.

50/51 In a realm of green: In front of 28 Billyard Avenue House there's a dense jungle. *Côté vert : devant le 28 de Billyard Avenue croît une jungle épaisse.* Im grünen Bereich: Vor dem 28 Billyard Avenue House wächst dichter Dschungel.

52/53 Design, through and through: living and dining room of the Katon Residence. *Design, double et triple : séjour et salle à manger de la résidence Katon.* Design, doppelt und dreifach: Wohn- und Esszimmer der Katon Residence.

54/55 High-end kitchenette: bright eating area right next to the kitchen. *Coin cuisine luxueux : à côté de la cuisine commence le lumineux espace salle à manger.* Edle Kochnische: Neben der Küche beginnt der helle Essbereich.

56/57 Twins in red: tulip chairs from Eero Saarinen in the Katon Residence. *Jumelles rouges : chaises tulipe d'Eero Saarinen dans la résidence Katon.* Zwillinge in Rot: Tulip-Stühle von Eero Saarinen in der Katon Residence.

58/59 A daring colour scheme: violet carpet and black parquet flooring in Bolland House. *Le courage de la couleur : tapis violet et parquet noir dans la maison Bolland.* Mut zur Farbe: Violetter Teppich und schwarzes Parkett im Bolland House.

60/61 Just like in the tropics: the inner garden of the Marshall Residence in a suburb of Sydney. *Comme dans les tropiques : jardin intérieur de la résidence Marshall dans une banlieue de Sydney.* Wie in den Tropen: Innengarten der Marshall Residence in einem Vorort von Sydney.

62/63 Open Space: what used to be a carriage factory is now Sam Marshall's dining room. *Impression d'usine : dans l' « open space » de Sam Marshall, on fabriquait autrefois des carrosses.* Fabrikflair: Im „open space" von Sam Marshall wurden einst Kutschen hergestellt.

64/65 Won't you sit down? Living room and dining room with furniture by Eames and Saarinen. *Prenez place : espace séjour et salle à manger avec des meubles d'Eames et Saarinen.* Nehmen Sie Platz: Wohn- und Essbereich mit Möbeln von Eames und Saarinen.

66/67 Homage to Asia: pebble garden at the Markham/Qasabian Residence. *Hommage à l'Asie : jardin de gravier dans la résidence Markham/Qasabian.* Hommage an Asien: Kieselsteingarten vor der Markham/Qasabian Residence.

68/69 Tea hour: Christina Markham and Rita Qasabian appreciate simple ambience. *L'heure du thé : Christina Markham et Rita Qasabian apprécient les ambiances sobres.* Teestunde: Christina Markham und Rita Qasabian schätzen schlichtes Ambiente.

70/71 Scandinavian classics: in the open living area of the Markham/Qasabian Residence. *Classique scandinave : dans l'espace séjour ouvert de la résidence Markham/Qasabian.* Skandinavische Klassiker: Im offenen Wohnbereich der Markham/Qasabian Residence.

72/73 Light and dark: a futon and chair by Eames in the Markham/Qasabian Residence. *Le clair et le sombre : futon et fauteuil d'Eames dans la résidence Markham/Qasabian.* Hell und dunkel: Futon und ein Sessel von Eames in der Markham/Qasabian Residence.

74/75 Pure inspiration: Christina Markham and Rita Qasabian's study. *Inspiration pure : le bureau de Christina Markham et Rita Qasabian.* Inspiration pur: Das Arbeitszimmer von Christina Markham und Rita Qasabian.

76/77 Twilight hour: the stone garden with pool at the Gibbeson/Litynski House. *Heure bleue : jardin de pierre et bassin d'eau de la maison Gibbeson/Litynski.* Blaue Stunde: Der Steingarten mit Wasserbecken im Gibbeson/Litynski House.

78/79 Bedside art: the bedroom of the Gibbeson/Litynski House. *L'art autour du lit : chambre à coucher de la maison Gibbeson/Litynski.* Kunst am Bett: Schlafzimmer des Gibbeson/Litynski House.

80/81 Green accents: in the refined living room of Linda Gregoriou and Dale Jones-Evans. *Notes vertes : dans le salon raffiné de Linda Gregoriou et Dale Jones-Evans.* Grüne Akzente: Im raffinierten Wohnzimmer von Linda Gregoriou und Dale Jones-Evans.

82/83 Sleeping on silk: Gregoriou and Jones-Evans brought the fabric from Japan. *Sommeil soyeux : les étoffes ont été rapportées du Japon par Gregoriou et Jones-Evans.* Schlafen auf Seide: Die Stoffe haben Gregoriou und Jones-Evans aus Japan mitgebracht.

84/85 Living by the water: the enchanting patio of the Adams House by Alex Popov. *Habiter au bord de l'eau : dans le merveilleux patio de la maison Adam d'Alex Popov.* Wohnen am Wasser: Im zauberhaften Patio des Adams House von Alex Popov.

86/87 Ascending: Alex Popov connects the living room and sleeping area with these stairs. *Elévation : par cet escalier, Alex Popov réunit l'espace séjour et chambre à coucher.* Aufstrebend: Über diese Treppe verbindet Alex Popov Wohn- und Schlafbereich.

88/89 In white and light brown: Alex Popov's dining room with a table by Alvar Aalto. *En blanc et brun clair : la salle à manger d'Alex Popov avec une table d'Alvar Aalto.* In Weiß und Hellbraun: Alex Popovs Esszimmer mit einem Tisch von Alvar Aalto.

90/91 Broad surface: Alex Popov had the wood for the counter sent from Canada. *Grande surface : c'est du Canada qu'Alex Popov a fait venir le bois du comptoir.* Weite Fläche: Das Holz für den Tresen ließ Alex Popov aus Kanada kommen.

92/93 Artistic: a work of Peter Francis Lawrence in Bay Watch House. *Artistique : une œuvre de Peter Francis Lawrence dans la maison Bay Watch.* Kunstvoll: Ein Werk von Peter Francis Lawrence im Bay Watch House.

94/95 Lots of room to eat: at Xavier House, designed by Alex Popov. *Beaucoup d'espace pour manger : dans la maison Xavier, dessinée par Alex Popov.* Viel Raum zum Essen: Im Xavier House, entworfen von Alex Popov.

96/97 Flooded with light: the gleaming white bedroom of Xavier House. *Blanc radieux : la chambre à coucher inondée de lumière de la maison Xavier.* Strahlend weiß: Das lichtdurchflutete Schlafzimmer des Xavier House.

98/99 Private pool: in front of Xavier House – with a view of the Mosman quarter. *Piscine privée : devant la maison Xavier – avec vue sur le quartier Mosman.* Privater Pool: Vor dem Xavier House im Viertel Mosman.

100/101 Colourful sunloungers: by the pool of the Levisohn House in Greenwich. *Chaises longues colorées : près de la piscine de la maison Levisohn à Greenwich.* Bunte Sonnenliegen: Am Pool des Levisohn House in Greenwich.

102/103 Delicate colours: In the Levisohn House, the living room and dining room run together. *Teintes douces : dans la maison Levisohn, transition imperceptible entre le séjour et la salle à manger.* Zarte Farben: Im Levisohn House gehen Wohn- und Esszimmer ineinander über.

104/105 Rare piece: The sofa in this living room was upholstered in elephant skin. *Pièce rare : le canapé de ce salon est recouvert de peau d'éléphant.* Seltenes Stück: Das Sofa in diesem Wohnzimmer wurde mit Elefantenhaut bezogen.

106/107 Clearly divided: Behind the kitchen a narrow staircase leads to the upper story. *Séparation claire : derrière la cuisine, un escalier étroit conduit à l'étage supérieur.* Klar getrennt: Hinter der Küche führt eine schmale Treppe ins Obergeschoss.

108/109 Light reflections: The wooden venetian blinds ensure comfort and warmth. *Reflets de lumière : la jalousie en bois crée un effet de légèreté et de chaleur.* Lichtreflexe: Die hölzerne Jalousie sorgt für Leichtigkeit und Wärme.

110/111 Beautifully textured wood: the stairs in the English House. *Bois bien structuré : escalier dans la maison English.* Schön strukturiertes Holz: Treppe im English House.

112/113 For friends: Mitchell and Helen English serve delicacies from Turkey. *Pour les amis : Mitchell et Helen English servent des spécialités turques.* Für Freunde: Mitchell und Helen English servieren Köstlichkeiten aus der Türkei.

114/115 A place to dream: a blue armchair from the '50s in the living room of the English House. *Place aux rêves : un fauteuil bleu des années 50 dans le salon des English.* Platz zum Träumen: Ein blauer Sessel aus den 50ern im Wohnzimmer des English House.

116/117 The language of art: in the dining room of gallery owner Kerry Crowley. *Le langage de l'art : dans la salle à manger de la galeriste Kerry Crowley.* Die Sprache der Kunst: Im Esszimmer der Galeristin Kerry Crowley.

118/119 Modern country style: cosy sofas in front of Kerry Crowley's fireplace. *Style country moderne : canapé confortable devant la cheminée de Kerry Crowley.* Moderner Countrystil: Gemütliche Sofas vor dem Kamin von Kerry Crowley.

120/121 As high as the ceiling: a picture by Imants Tillers in Kerry Crowley's music room. *Haut comme la pièce : un tableau d'Imants Tillers dans la pièce de musique de Kerry Crowley.* Raumhoch: Ein Bild von Imants Tillers in Kerry Crowleys Musikzimmer.

122/123 Time to read: the living room of the Stone/Gale House in the suburb of Chippendale. *Le temps de lire : salon de la maison Stone/Gale House dans la banlieue de Chippendale.* Zeit zum Lesen: Wohnzimmer des Stone/Gale House im Vorort Chippendale.

124/125 A direct view: The elegant living room looks directly onto the terrace and nature. *Vue imprenable : l'élégant salon donne directement sur la terrasse et la nature.* Durchblick: Vom eleganten Wohnzimmer sieht man direkt auf die Terrasse und die Natur.

126/127 Brilliant combination: Dark parquet flooring and furniture with clear forms. *Brillante affaire : parquet sombre et mobilier aux formes claires.* Glänzende Angelegenheit: Dunkles Parkett und Möbel mit klaren Formen.

128/129 Scandinavia meets Sydney: classics around a table by Norman/ Quaine. *La Scandinavie à la rencontre de Sydney : musiciens autour d'une table de Norman/Quaine.* Skandinavien meets Sydney: Klassiker rund um einen Tisch von Norman/Quaine.

130/131 Like a laboratory: the kitchen in white corian in the Stone/Gale House. *Propice au travail : la cuisine de corian blanc dans la maison Stone/Gale.* Labor-like: Die Küche aus weißem Corian im Stone/Gale House.

"On the balcony there was a white plastic table (that looked like a Saarinen design) and eight red scratched-up artificial leather chairs that had been thrown out by the Cho-How Dumpling House."

Peter Carey in *30 Days in Sydney, A Wildly Distorted Account*

« Sur le balcon se dressait une table en plastique blanc (qui ressemblait à une maquette de Saarinen) et huit chaises rouges en similicuir égratigné, mises au rebut devant la maison Cho-How Dumpling. »

Peter Carey dans *Gebrauchsanweisung für Sydney*

„Auf dem Balkon standen ein weißer Plastiktisch (der wie ein Entwurf von Saarinen aussah) und acht zerschrammte rote Kunstlederstühle, die vom Cho-How Dumpling House ausrangiert worden waren."

Peter Carey in *Gebrauchsanweisung für Sydney*

CHARMING DETAILS

Détails charmants Charmante Details

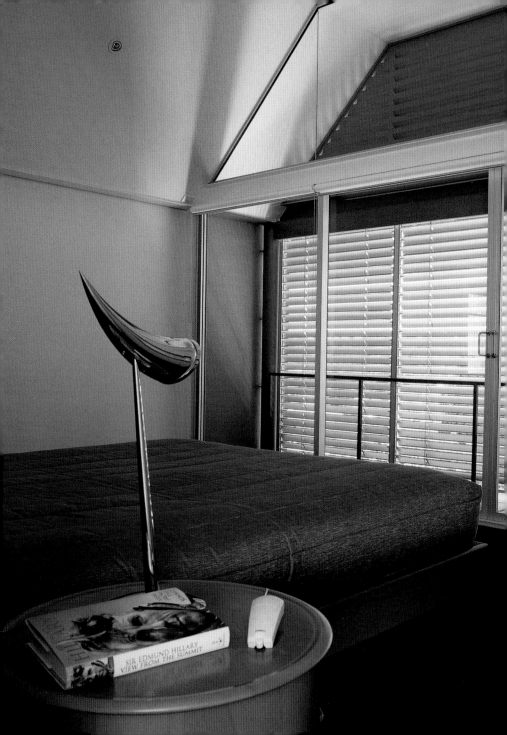

138 You've got mail: gleaming mailbox at the entrance. *Du courrier pour vous : boîtes à lettres étince lantes à l'entrée de la maison.* Post für Sie: Glänzende Brief kästen am Eingang.

140 Structured: two armchairs in the bed room of the Archer House. *Structurés : deux fauteuils dans la chambre à coucher de la maison Archer.* Strukturiert: Zwei Ses sel im Schlafzimmer des Archer House.

141 Place of honour: the "Y's" chair by Christophe Pillet in the Reynolds House. *Place d'honneur : la chaise « Y's » de Christophe Pillet dans la maison Reynolds.* Ehrenplatz: Der Stuhl „Y's" von Christophe Pillet im Reynolds House.

142 Still life in white: porcelain from De De Ce on a shelf by Dur bach Block. *Nature morte en blanc : porcelaine de De De Ce sur une étagère de Durbach Block.* Still leben in Weiß: Porzel lan von De De Ce auf einem Regal von Dur bach Block.

144 Trio: stools by Space in the kitchen of Bay Watch House. *Par trois : tabourets de Space dans la cuisine de la maison Bay Watch.* Dreier gruppe: Hocker von Space in der Küche des Bay Watch House.

145 Black granite: in the bathroom of Bay Watch House. *Granit noir : dans la salle de bain de la maison Bay Watch.* Schwarzer Granit: Im Badezimmer des Bay Watch House.

146 Chrome and glass: the minimalist kitchen of the Markham/Qasabian Residence. *Chrome et verre : la cuisine mini maliste de la résidence. Markham/Qasabian.* Chrom und Glas: Die minimalistische Küche der Markham/Qasa bian Residence.

148 Little labyrinth: in the hallway of Bay Watch House. *Petit labyrinthe : dans la pièce de passage de la maison Bay Watch.* Kleines Labyrinth: Im Durchgangszimmer des Bay Watch House.

149 Best position: in the bedroom of Bay Watch House. *En excellente position : dans la chambre à coucher de la maison Bay Watch.* In bester Lage: Im Schlafzim mer des Bay Watch House.

150 Vanishing point: Sam Marshall's hidden roof terrace. *Point de fuite : la terrasse cachée sur le toit de Sam Marshall.* Fluchtpunkt: Die versteckte Dachterrasse von Sam Marshall.

152 Classic examples: ceramics collection of Mitchell and Helen English. *Exemplaires modèles : collection de céramiques de Mitchell et Helen English.* Musterbeispiele: Keramiksammlung von Mitchell und Helen English.

153 Table for two: on the little terrace of the Gibbeson/Litynski House. *Table pour deux : sur la petite terrasse de la maison Gibbeson/Litynski.* Table for two: Auf der kleinen Terrasse des Gibbeson/Litynski House.

154 Maritime accessories: model ship in the bedroom. *Accessoires maritimes : maquette de bateau dans la chambre à coucher.* Maritimes Accessoire: Modellschiff im Schlafzimmer.

156 Geometry: wall detail in the Markham/Qasabian Residence. *Géométrie : détail mural dans la résidence Markham/ Qasabian.* Geometrie: Wanddetail in der Markham/ Qasabian Residence.

157 Stone on stone: at the home of Christina Markham and Rita Qasabian. *Pierre sur pierre : chez Christina Markham et Rita Qasabian.* Stein auf Stein: Bei Christina Markham und Rita Qasabian.

158 Mask-like: by Sam Marshall's bed. *Masqué : à côté du lit de Sam Marshall.* Maskenhaft: Am Bett von Sam Marshall.

160 Sliding door: That is how Sam Marshall separates the living room from the stairwell. *Porte coulissante : c'est ainsi que Sam Marshall sépare le séjour de l'escalier.* Schiebetür: So trennt Sam Marshall Wohnraum und Treppenhaus.

161 Of glass and synthetic resin: vases in the Marshall Residence. *Verre et résine artificielle : vases de la résidence Marshall.* Aus Glas und Kunstharz: Vasen in der Marshall Residence.

162 Famous photographer: a portrait made by Bill Henson. *Photographe célèbre : un portrait réalisé par Bill Henson.* Berühmter Fotograf: Ein Portrait made by Bill Henson.

164 Authentically old: The Stone/Gale House has original blackbutt floorboards. *Authentiquement ancien : la maison Stone/Gale possède un parquet original en blackbutt.* Echt alt: Das Stone/ Gale House besitzt originale Blackbutt-Dielen.

165 In miniature: unusual objets d'art in the Stone/Gale House. *En miniature : objets d'art insolites dans la maison Stone/Gale.* En miniature: Ungewöhnliche Kunstgegenstände im Stone/ Gale House.

166 Locked away: red metal cupboards at Sam Marshall's. *Fermées : armoires rouges en métal chez Sam Marshall.* Verschlossen: Rote Metallschränke bei Sam Marshall.

168 Bon appétit: at the table of Mitchell and Helen English. *Bon appétit : à table chez Mitchell et Helen English.* Guten Appetit: Am Tisch von Mitchell und Helen English.

169 Colour play: In the kitchen of the English House. *Jeux de couleur : dans la cuisine de la maison English.* Farbspiele: In der Küche des English House.

170 Brilliant orange: a vase by Dinosaur Designs in the English House. *Orange lumineux : un vase de Dinosaur Designs chez les English.* Leuchtend orange: Eine Vase von Dinosaur Designs im English House.

172 Successful mixture: the dining table of the Ormandy/Olsen House. *Mélange réussi : table à manger de la maison Ormandy/ Olse.* Gelungene Mischung: Esstisch des Ormandy/Olsen House.

173 Fresh ingredients: in the kitchen of the Ormandy/Olsen House. *Ingrédients frais : dans la cuisine de la maison Ormandy/ Olsen.* Frische Zutaten: In der Küche des Ormandy/Olsen House.

174 Endearingly chaotic: at Kerry Crowley's. *Charmant chaos : chez Kerry Crowley.* Liebenswert chaotisch: Bei Kerry Crowley.

176 Artificial communication: an object by Robert MacPherson. *Communication artificielle : un objet de Robert MacPherson.* Künstliche Kommunikation: Ein Objekt von Robert MacPherson.

177 On bird feet: shining gold cups by Sandra Taylor at Kerry Crowley's. *Sur pattes d'oiseau : gobelets aux reflets dorés de Sandra Taylor chez Kerry Crowley.* Auf Vogelfüßen: Goldglänzende Becher von Sandra Taylor bei Kerry Crowley.

178 Working efficiently: coffee machine by Pavoni. *Efficace : machine à café de Pavoni.* Funktionstüchtig: Kaffeemaschine von Pavoni.

180 At their best: vases by Dinosaur Designs in the Ormandy/Olsen House. *Floraison : vases de Dinosaur Designs dans la maison Ormandy/Olsen.* Blütezeit: Vasen von Dinosaur Designs im Ormandy/Olsen House.

181 Striped and in 3-D: a painted sculpture by Simeon Nelson. *Rayée et en 3-D : une sculpture-portrait de Simeon Nelson.* Gestreift und in 3-D: Eine Gemäldeskulptur von Simeon Nelson.

182 Memory: wooden console from the '50s in the Hipgrave/Waring House. *Souvenir : console en bois des années 50 dans la maison Hipgrave/Waring.* Erinnerung: Holzkonsole aus den 50ern im Hipgrave/Waring House.

184 Open kitchen: in the Bolland House above Balmoral Beach. *Cuisine ouverte : dans la maison Bolland au-dessus de Balmoral Beach.* Offene Küche: Im Bolland House über dem Balmoral Beach.

185 Tapering to a point: light by Philippe Starck in the Bolland House. *Pointu : luminaire de Philippe Starck dans la maison Bolland.* Spitz zulaufend: Leuchte von Philippe Starck im Bolland House.

186 Fanned out: Verner-Panton Lamp in the English House. *Ouvert en éventail : lampe Verner-Panton chez les English.* Aufgefächert: Verner-Panton-Lampe im English House.

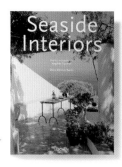

Berlin Interiors
Ed. Angelika Taschen / Ingeborg Wiensowski / Hardcover, 320 pp. / € 29.99 / $ 39.99 / £ 24.99 / ¥ 5.900

Miami Interiors
Ed. Angelika Taschen / Patricia Parinejad / Hardcover, 320 pp. / € 29.99 / $ 39.99 / £ 24.99 / ¥ 5.900

Seaside Interiors
Ed. Angelika Taschen / Diane Dorrans Saeks / Hardcover, 304 pp. / € 29.99 / $ 39.99 / £ 24.99 / ¥ 5.900

"...an elegant and enlightening addition for any coffee table." —Homes & Living, Perth, on Berlin Interiors

"Buy them all and add some pleasure to your life."